JAZZ HYMNS

Arranged by Larry E. Newman

MW00892163

LIST OF HYMNS

Mighty Fortress is Our God............. ...2	Now Thank We All Our God.................22
mazing Grace....................................4	Praise God From Whom All Blessings Flow.24
e Thou My Vision...............................6	Swing Low, Sweet Chariot...................26
ome, Thou Long-Expected Jesus.............8	The Old Rugged Cross.......................28
rown Him With Many Crowns.................10	Thine Is the Glory............................30
reat Is Thy Faithfulness......................12	To God Be the Glory.........................32
ow Great Thou Art.............................14	Turn Your Eyes Upon Jesus................34
esus Christ Is Risen Today...................16	We Gather Together..........................36
esus Loves Me.................................18	What a Friend We Have In Jesus..........38
oyful, Joyful, We Adore Thee................20	When I Survey the Wondrous Cross......40

ONLINE AUDIO

Discover **Jazz Hymns** – where cherished hymns meet the vibrant world of jazz! Immerse yourself in the timeless essence of twenty beloved hymns, now adorned with sophisticated jazz harmonies, designed to be easily performed by piano enthusiasts of all levels.

This unique collection features classics like 'Amazing Grace,' 'How Great Thou Art,' and 'What a Friend We Have in Jesus,' each thoughtfully arranged to blend tradition with the allure of contemporary jazz. Featuring beautiful arrangements, online audio mp3s and included lyrics, this book is a comprehensive resource for both pianists and congregations alike.

A Mighty Fortress is Our God

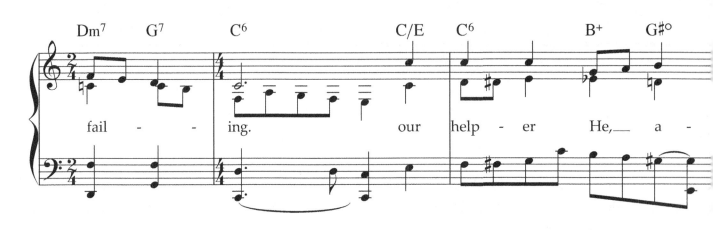

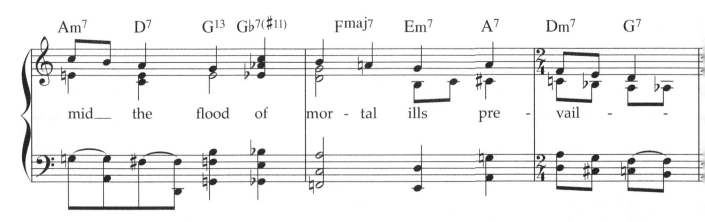

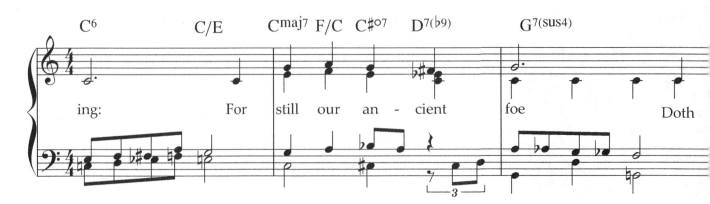

A mighty fortress is our God,
A bulwark never failing;
Our helper He, amid the flood
Of mortal ills prevailing:
For still our ancient foe
Doth seek to work us woe;
His craft and power are great,
And, armed with cruel hate,
On earth is not his equal.

And though this world, with devils filled,
Should threaten to undo us,
We will not fear, for God hath willed
His truth to triumph through us:
The Prince of Darkness grim,
We tremble not for him;
His rage we can endure,
For lo! his doom is sure,
One little word shall fell him.

Amazing Grace

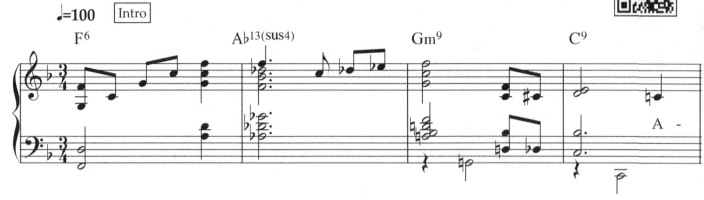

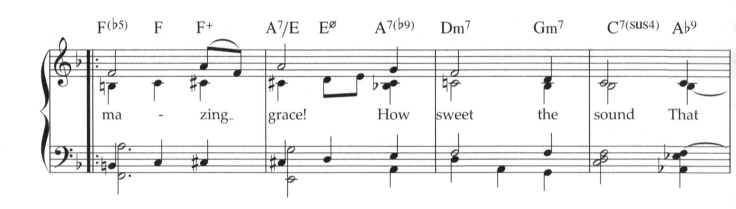

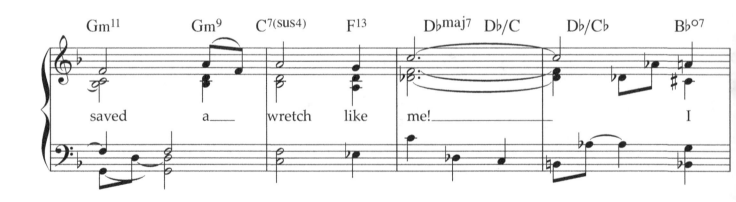

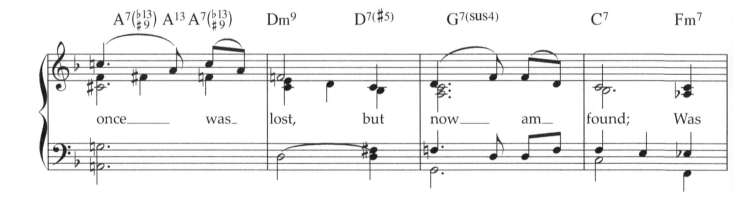

5

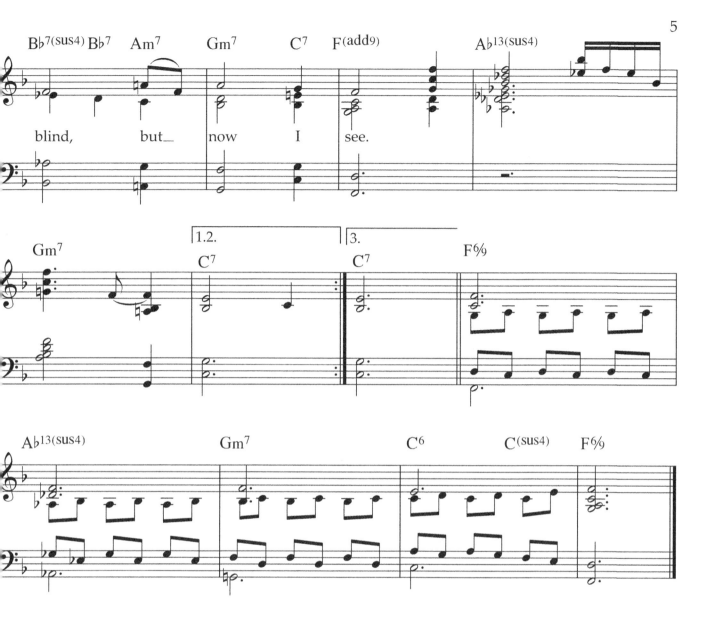

Amazing grace! How sweet the sound,
That saved a wretch like me!
I once was lost, but now am found;
Was blind, but now I see.

'Twas grace that taught my heart to fear,
And grace my fears relieved;
How precious did that grace appear
The hour I first believed.

Through many dangers, toils, and snares,
I have already come;
'Tis grace hath brought me safe thus far,
And grace will lead me home.

The Lord has promised good to me,
His Word my hope secures;
He will my Shield and Portion be,
As long as life endures.

Yea, when this flesh and heart shall fail,
And mortal life shall cease,
I shall possess, within the veil,
A life of joy and peace.

The Lord has promised good to me,
His Word my hope secures;
He will my Shield and Portion be,
As long as life endures

Be Thou My Vision

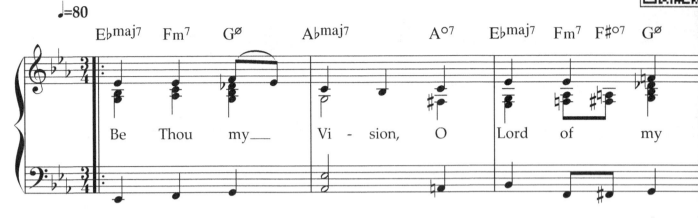

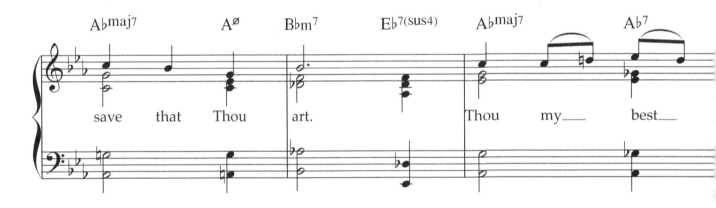

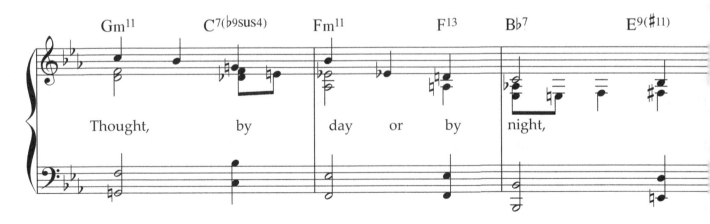

Be Thou my Vision, O Lord of my heart;
Naught be all else to me, save that Thou art.
Thou my best Thought, by day or by night,
Waking or sleeping, Thy presence my light.

Be Thou my wisdom, and Thou my true Word;
I ever with Thee and Thou with me, Lord;
Thou my great Father, I Thy true son;
Thou in me dwelling, and I with Thee one.

Riches I heed not, nor man's empty praise,
Thou mine inheritance, now and always;
Thou and Thou only, first in my heart,
High King of Heaven, my Treasure Thou art.

High King of heaven, my victory won
May I reach heaven's joys, O bright heaven's sun
Heart of my own heart, whatever befall
Still be my vision, O ruler of all.

Come, Thou Long-Expected Jesus

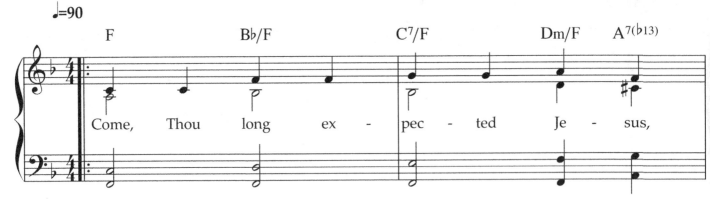

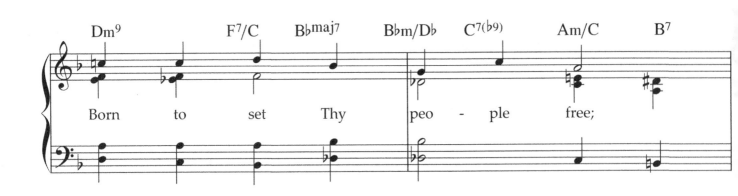

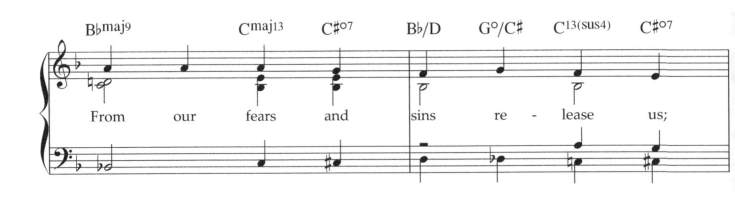

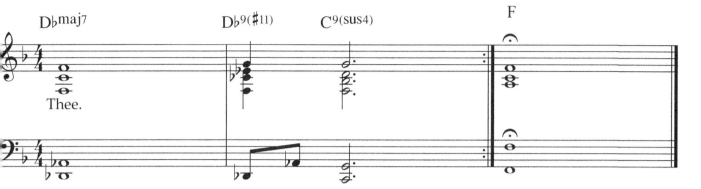

Come, Thou long expected Jesus,
Born to set Thy people free;
From our fears and sins release us;
Let us find our rest in Thee.
Israel's strength and consolation,
Hope of all the earth Thou art;
Dear Desire of ev'ry nation,
Joy of every longing heart.

Joy to those who long to see Thee
Day-spring from on high, appear.
Come, Thou promised Rod of Jesse,
Of Thy birth, we long to hear!
O'er the hills the angels singing
News, glad tidings of a birth;
"Go to Him your praises bringing
Christ the Lord has come to earth!"

Come to earth to taste our sadness,
He whose glories knew no end.
By His life He brings us gladness,
Our redeemer, Shepherd, Friend.
Leaving riches without number,
Born within a cattle stall;
This the everlasting wonder,
Christ was born the Lord of all.

Born Thy people to deliver,
Born a child, and yet a King,
Born to reign in us for ever,
Now Thy gracious kingdom bring.
By Thine own eternal Spirit
Rule in all our hearts alone;
By Thine all-sufficient merit
Raise us to Thy glorious throne.

Crown Him With Many Crowns

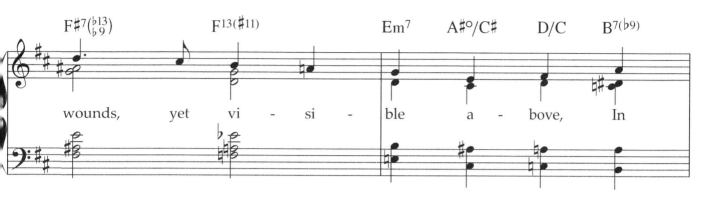

wounds, yet vi - si - ble a - bove, In

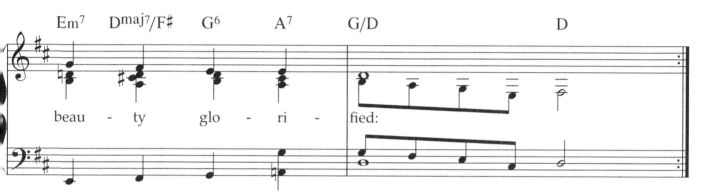

beau - ty glo - ri - fied:

Crown Him with many crowns,
The Lamb upon His throne;
Hark! how the heav'nly anthem drowns
All music but its own!
Awake, my soul, and sing
Of Him who died for thee,
And hail Him as thy matchless King
Through all eternity.

Crown Him the Virgin's Son,
The God Incarnate born,
Whose arm those crimson trophies won
Which now His brow adorn:
Fruit of the mystic Tree,
As of that Tree the Stem;
The Root whence flows Thy mercy free,
The Babe of Bethlehem.

Crown Him the Lord of Love:
Behold His hands and side;
Rich wounds yet visible above
In beauty glorified:
No angel in the sky
Can fully bear that sight,
But downward bends his burning eye
At mysteries so bright.

Great Is Thy Faithfulness

♩=90

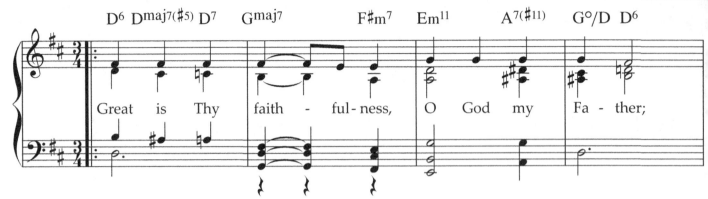

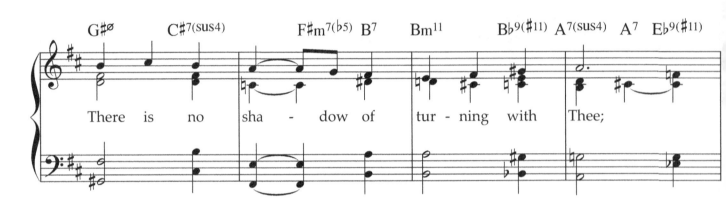

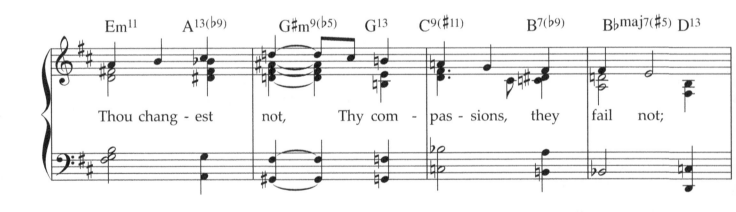

Great is Thy faithfulness, O God my Father;
ere is no shadow of turning with Thee;
ou changest not, Thy compassions, they fail not;
Thou hast been, Thou forever wilt be.

frain:

eat is Thy faithfulness! Great is Thy faithfulness!
orning by morning new mercies I see;
I have needed Thy hand hath provided:
eat is Thy faithfulness, Lord, unto me!

Summer and winter, and springtime and harvest;
sun, moon, and stars in their courses above
join with all nature in manifold witness
to Thy great faithfulness, mercy, and love.
[Refrain]

Pardon for sin and a peace that endureth,
Thine own dear presence to cheer and to guide;
strength for today and bright hope for tomorrow:
blessings all mine, with ten thousand beside
[Refrain]

How Great Thou Art

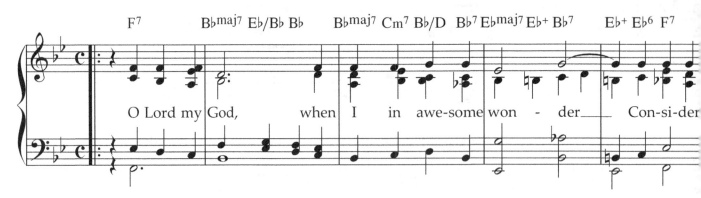

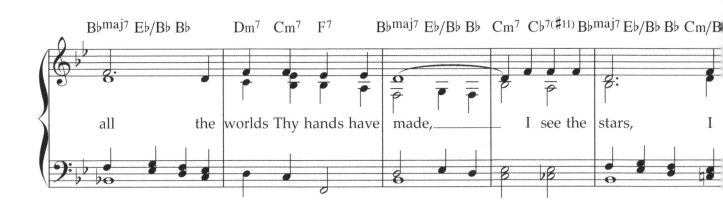

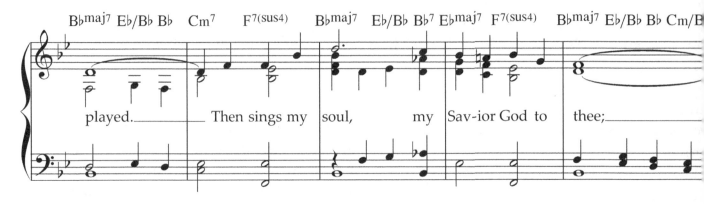

Oh Lord, my God, When I, in awesome wonder
Consider all the worlds Thy hands have made
I see the stars, I hear the rolling thunder
Thy power throughout the universe displayed

Then sings my soul, my Savior God to Thee
How great Thou art, how great Thou art
Then sings my soul, my Savior God to Thee
How great Thou art, how great Thou art

And when I think that God, His Son not sparing
Sent Him to die, I scarce can take it in
That on the cross, my burden gladly bearing
He bled and died to take away my sin

Then sings my soul, my Savior God to Thee
How great Thou art, how great Thou art
Then sings my soul, my Savior God to Thee
How great Thou art, how great Thou art

When Christ shall come, with shout of acclamation
And take me home, what joy shall fill my heart
Then I shall bow, in humble adoration
And then proclaim, my God, how great Thou art

Then sings my soul, my Savior God to Thee
How great Thou art, how great Thou art
Then sings my soul, my Savior God to Thee
How great Thou art, how great Thou art

Jesus Christ Is Risen Today

♩=110

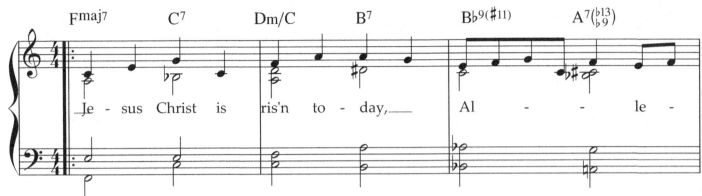

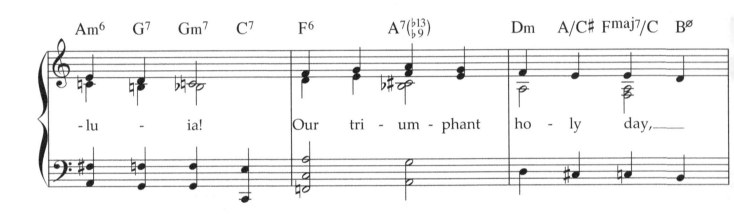

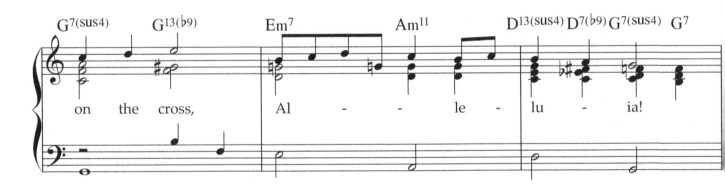

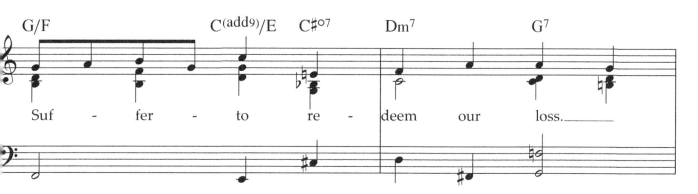

Chords: G/F   C^(add9)/E   C#°7   Dm7   G7

Suf - fer - to re - deem our loss._____

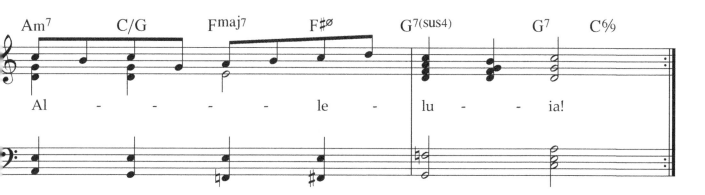

Chords: Am7   C/G   F^{maj7}   F#ø   G7(sus4)   G7   C6/9

Al - - - - le - lu - - ia!

Jesus Christ is risen today
Alleluia!
Our triumphant holy day
Alleluia!
Who did once upon the cross
Alleluia!
Suffer to redeem our loss
Alleluia!

Hymns of praise then let us sing
Alleluia!
Unto Christ, our heavenly king
Alleluia!
Who endured the cross and grave
Alleluia!
Sinners to redeem and save
Alleluia!

But the pains which He endured
Alleluia!
Our salvation have procured
Alleluia!
Now above the sky He's king
Alleluia!
Where the angels ever sing
Alleluia!

Jesus Loves Me

♩=90

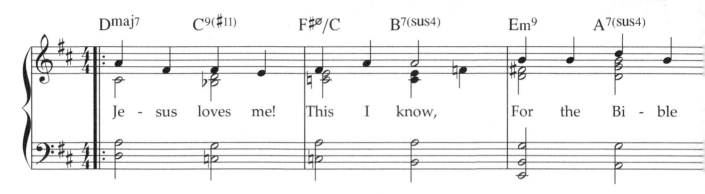

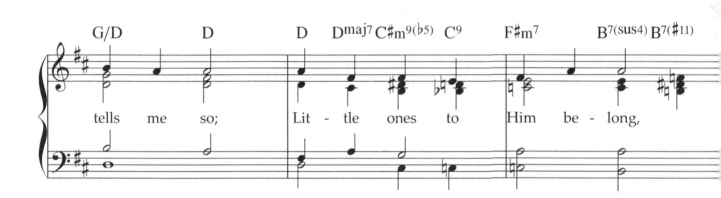

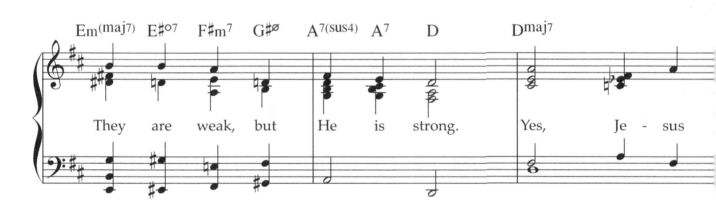

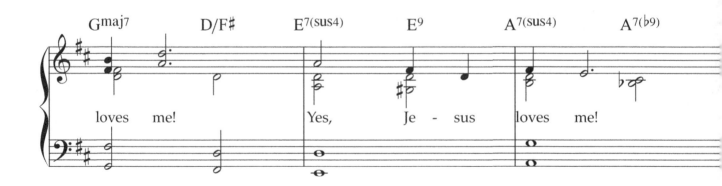

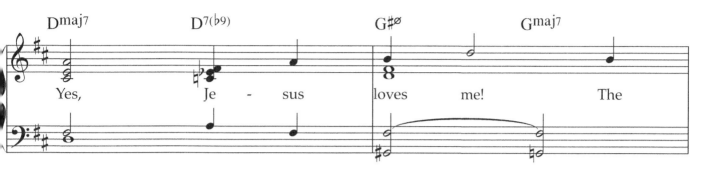

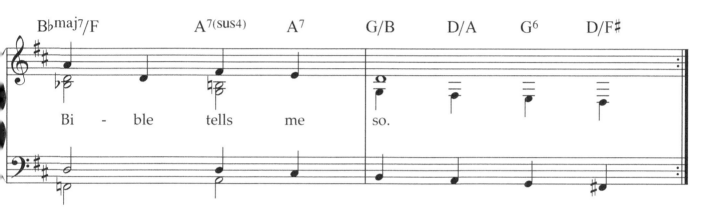

Jesus loves me, this I know,
for the Bible tells me so.
Little ones to him belong;
they are weak, but he is strong.

Yes, Jesus loves me! Yes, Jesus loves me!
Yes, Jesus loves me! The Bible tells me so.

 Jesus loves me he who died
heaven's gate to open wide.
He will wash away my sin,
let his little child come in.

Yes, Jesus loves me! Yes, Jesus loves me!
Yes, Jesus loves me! The Bible tells me so.

Jesus loves me, this I know,
as he loved so long ago,
taking children on his knee,
saying, "Let them come to me."

Yes, Jesus loves me! Yes, Jesus loves me!
Yes, Jesus loves me! The Bible tells me so.

Joyful, Joyful, We Adore Thee

♩=110 Intro

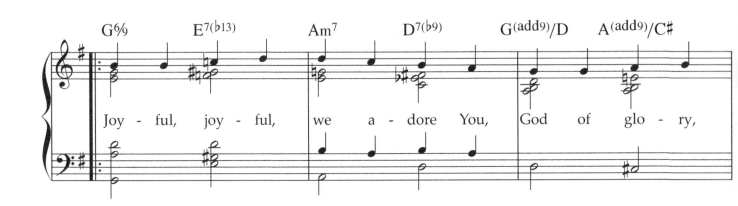

Joy - ful, joy - ful, we a - dore You, God of glo - ry,

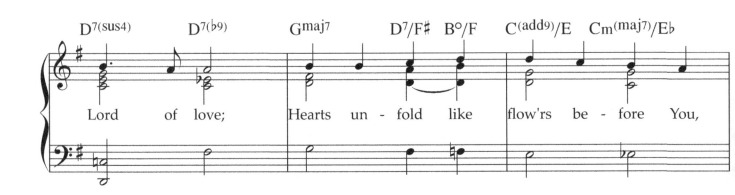

Lord of love; Hearts un - fold like flow'rs be - fore You,

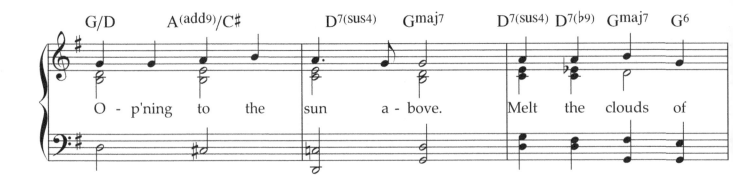

O - p'ning to the sun a - bove. Melt the clouds of

21

sin and sad - ness; Drive the dark of doubt a - way; Giv-

- er of im - mor - tal glad - ness, Fill us with the

light of day! day!

Joyful, joyful, we adore You,
God of glory, Lord of love;
Hearts unfold like flow'rs before You,
Op'ning to the sun above.
Melt the clouds of sin and sadness;
Drive the dark of doubt away;
Giver of immortal gladness,
Fill us with the light of day!

All Your works with joy surround You,
Earth and heav'n reflect Your rays,
Stars and angels sing around You,
Center of unbroken praise;
Field and forest, vale and mountain,
Flow'ry meadow, flashing sea,
Chanting bird and flowing fountain
Praising You eternally!

Always giving and forgiving,
Ever blessing, ever blest,
Well-spring of the joy of living,
Ocean-depth of happy rest!
Loving Father, Christ our Brother,
Let Your light upon us shine;
Teach us how to love each other,
Lift us to the joy divine.

Mortals, join the mighty chorus,
Which the morning stars began;
God's own love is reigning o'er us,
Joining people hand in hand.
Ever singing, march we onward,
Victors in the midst of strife;
Joyful music leads us sunward
In the triumph song of life.

Now Thank We All Our God

♩=90

Now thank we all our God with heart and hands and

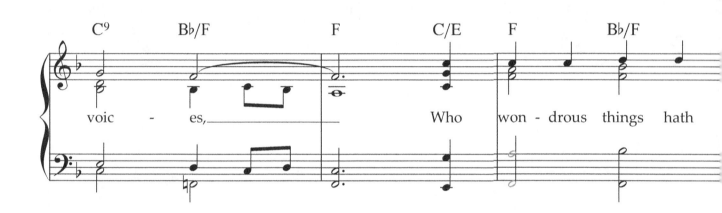

voic - es, Who won-drous things hath

done, In whom His world re - joic - es;

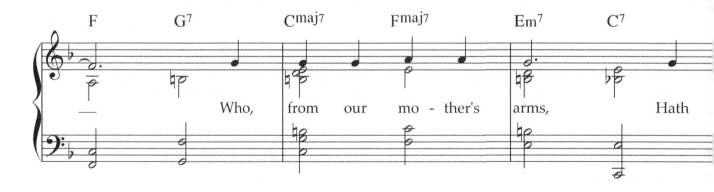

Who, from our mo - ther's arms, Hath

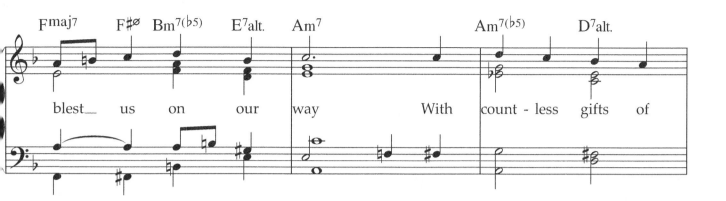

blest__ us on our way With count - less gifts of

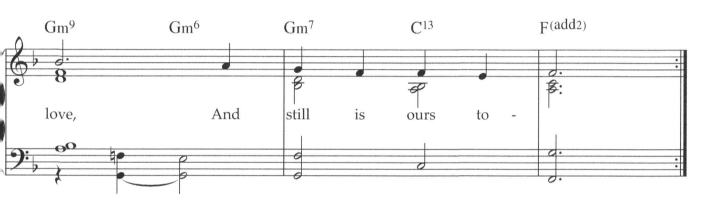

love, And still is ours to -

Now thank we all our God
with heart and hands and voices,
who wondrous things has done,
in whom his world rejoices;
who from our mothers' arms
has blessed us on our way
with countless gifts of love,
and still is ours today.

O may this bounteous God
through all our life be near us,
with ever joyful hearts
and blessed peace to cheer us,
to keep us in his grace,
and guide us when perplexed,
and free us from all ills
of this world in the next.

All praise and thanks to God
the Father now be given,
the Son and Spirit blest,
who reign in highest heaven
the one eternal God,
whom heaven and earth adore;
for thus it was, is now,
and shall be evermore.

Praise God From Whom All Blessings Flow

♩=100

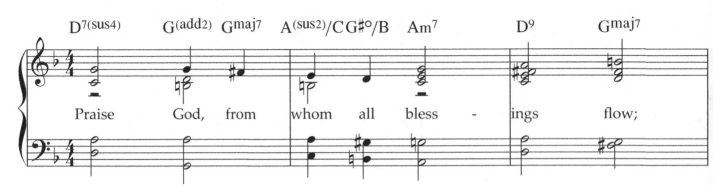

Praise God, from whom all bless - ings flow;

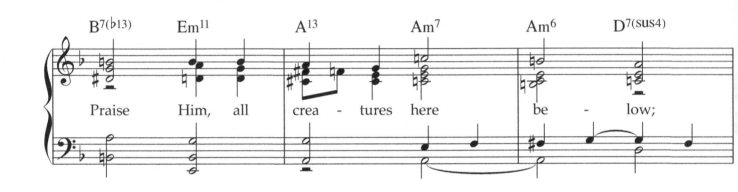

Praise Him, all crea - tures here be - low;

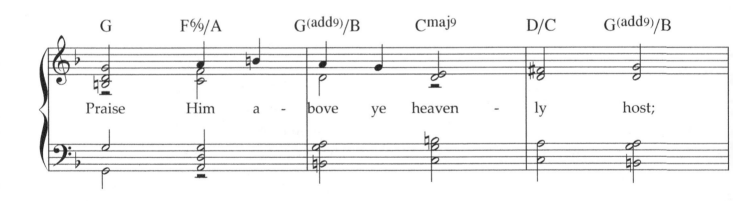

Praise Him a - bove ye heaven - ly host;

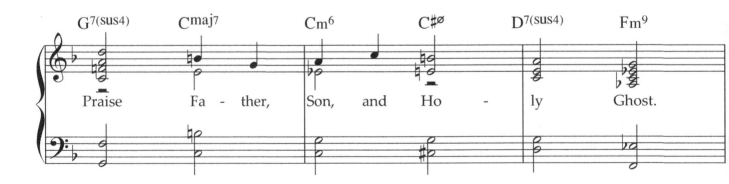

Praise Fa - ther, Son, and Ho - ly Ghost.

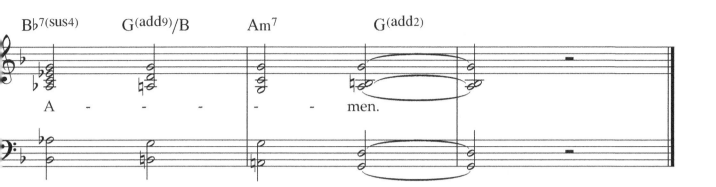

A - - - - - men.

Swing Low, Sweet Chariot

♩=100

Swing low, sweet char - i - ot___ com-ing for to car - ry me

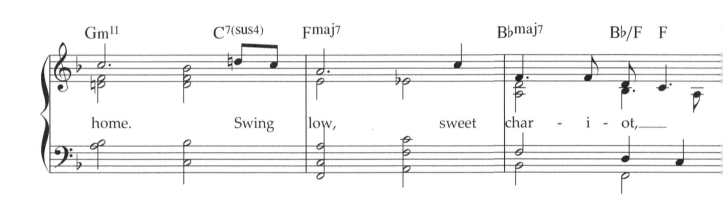

home. Swing low, sweet char - i - ot,___

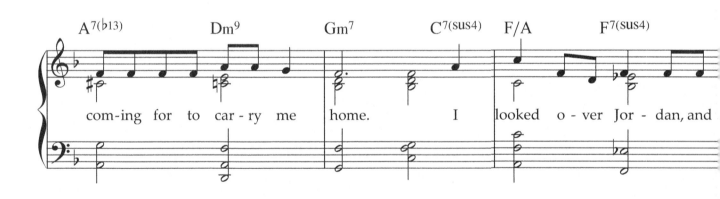

com-ing for to car - ry me home. I looked o - ver Jor - dan, and

what did I see?__ Com-ing for to car - ry me home. A

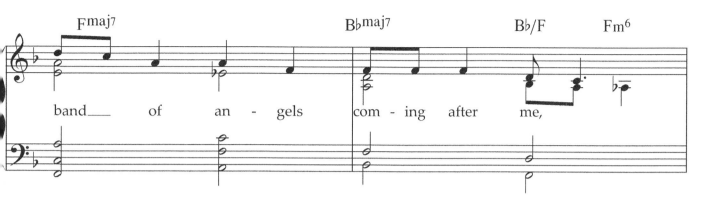

band___ of an - gels com - ing after me,

com - ing for to car - ry me home.

Swing low, sweet chariot
Coming for to carry me home
Swing low, sweet chariot
Coming for to carry he home

I looked over Jordan and what did I see
Coming for to carry he home
A band of angels coming after me
Coming for to carry me home

Swing low, sweet chariot
Coming for to carry me home
Swing low, sweet chariot
Coming for to carry me home

If you get there before I do
Coming for to carry me home
Tell all my friends I'm coming too
Coming for to carry me home

Swing low, sweet chariot
Coming for to carry me home
Swing low, sweet chariot
Coming for to carry me home

The Old Rugged Cross

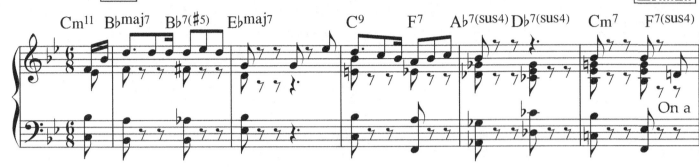

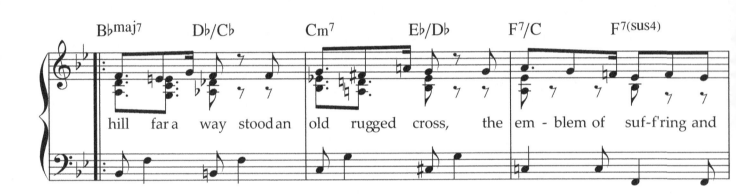

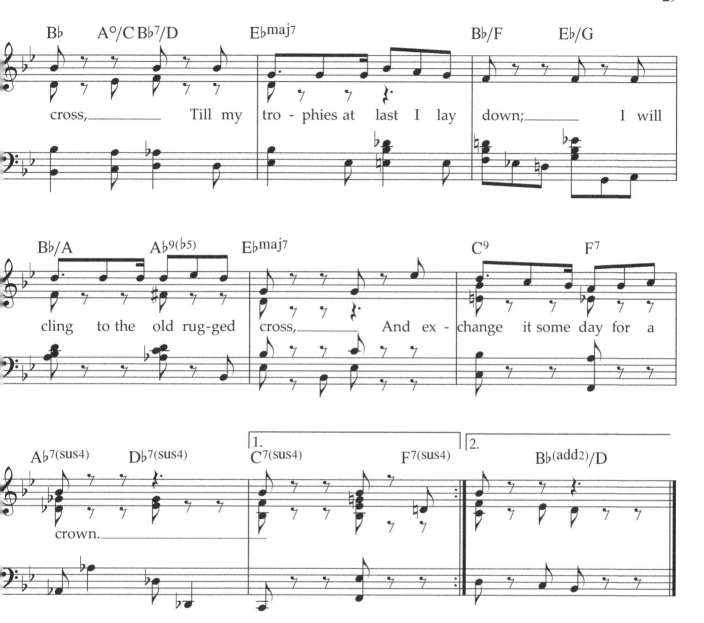

To the old rugged cross I will ever be true
It's shame and reproach gladly bear
Then he'll call me some day to my home far away
Where his glory forever I'll share

And I'll cherish the old rugged cross
Till my trophies at last I lay down
And I will cling to the old rugged cross
And exchange it some day for a crown

Thine Is the Glory

♩=100 Intro

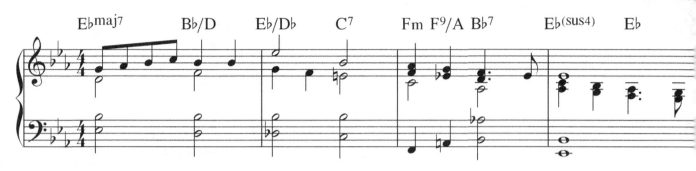

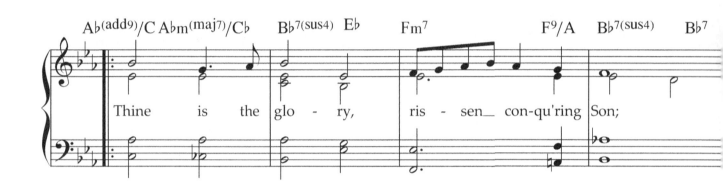

Thine is the glo - ry, ris - sen_ con-qu'ring Son;

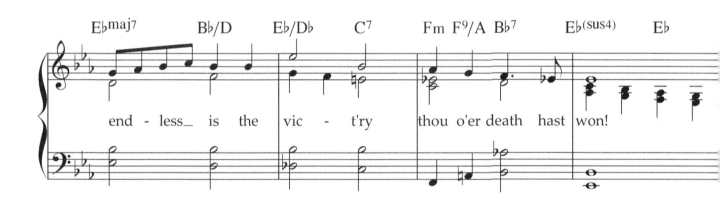

end - less_ is the vic - t'ry thou o'er death hast won!

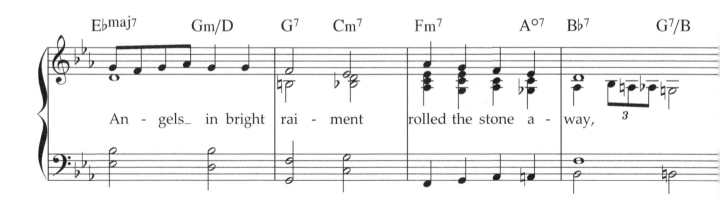

An - gels_ in bright rai - ment rolled the stone a - way,

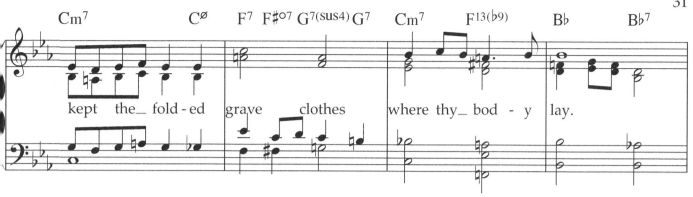

kept the_ fold - ed grave clothes where thy_ bod - y lay.

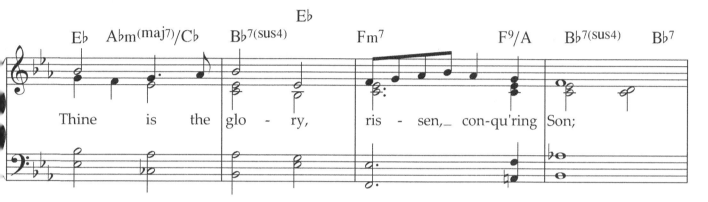

Thine is the glo - ry, ris - sen,_ con-qu'ring Son;

end - less_ is the vic - t'ry thou o'er death hast won!

No more we doubt Thee, glorious Prince of life!!
Life is nought without Thee; aid us in our strife;
make us more than conqu'rors, through Thy
deathless love;
bring us safe through Jordan to Thy home above.
[Refrain]

Thine be the glory, risen, conqu'ring Son;
endless is the vict'ry Thou o'er death hast won.
Angels in bright raiment rolled the stone away,
kept the folded grave-clothes where Thy body lay.

Refrain:
Thine be the glory, risen, conqu'ring Son;
endless is the vict'ry Thou o'er death hast won.

Lo! Jesus meets us, risen from the tomb.
Lovingly He greets us, scatters fear and gloom;
let His church with gladness hymns of triumph
sing,
for the Lord now liveth; death hath lost its sting.
[Refrain]

To God Be the Glory

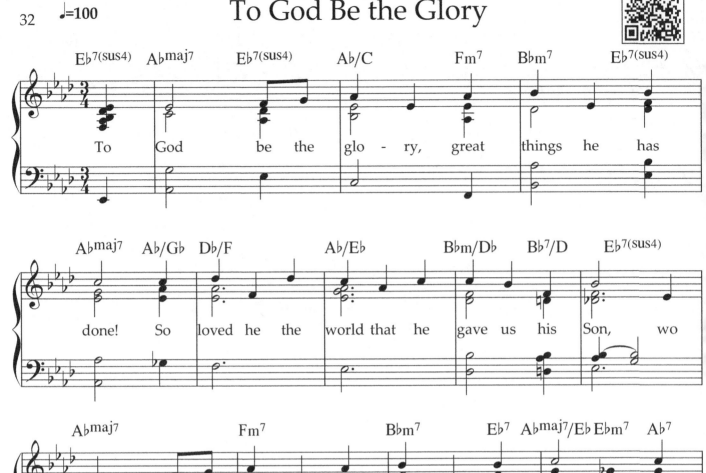

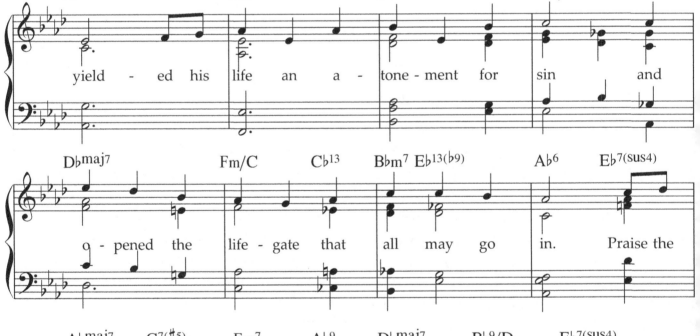

To God be the glory, great things He hath done,
So loved He the world that He gave us His Son,
Who yielded His life our redemption to win,
And opened the life-gate that all may go in.

Praise the Lord, praise the Lord,
Let the earth hear His voice;
Praise the Lord, praise the Lord,
Let the people rejoice;
Oh, come to the Father, through Jesus the Son,
And give Him the glory; great things He hath done.

To God be the glory, great things He hath done,
So loved He the world that He gave us His Son,
Who yielded His life our redemption to win,
And opened the life-gate that all may go in.

Oh, perfect redemption, the purchase of blood,
To every believer the promise of God;
The vilest offender who truly believes,
That moment from Jesus a pardon receives.

Turn Your Eyes Upon Jesus

♩=120

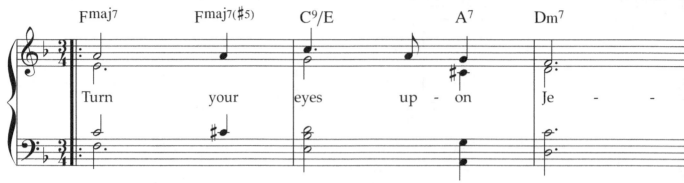

Turn your eyes up-on Je -

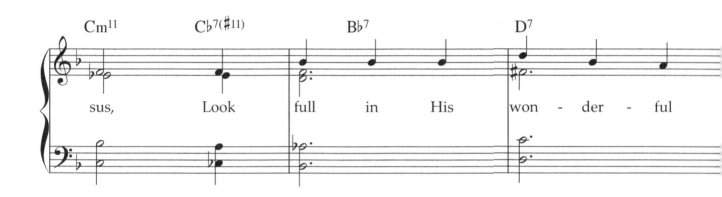

-sus, Look full in His won-der-ful

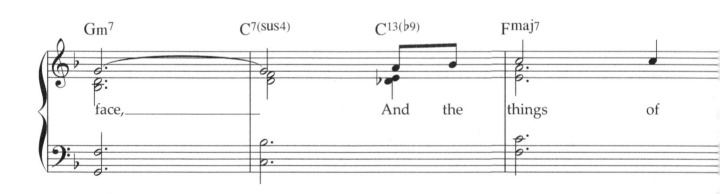

face,_____ And the things of

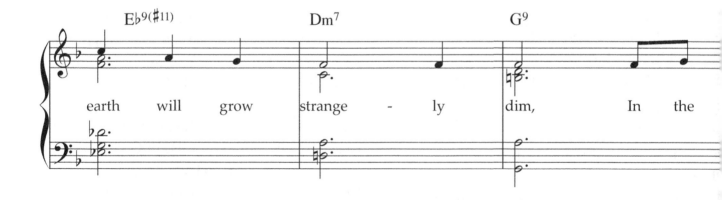

earth will grow strange-ly dim, In the

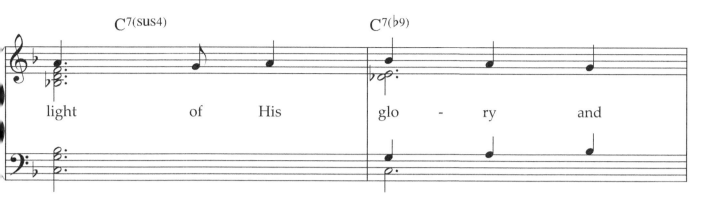

light   of   His   glo - ry   and

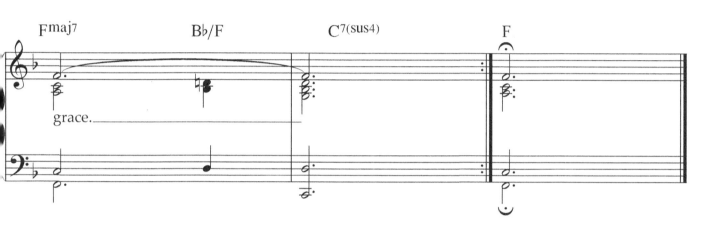

grace._____

soul are you weary and troubled
o light in the darkness you see
here's light for a look at the Savior
nd life more abundant and free

urn your eyes upon Jesus
ook full in his wonderful face
nd the things of earth will grow strangely dim
the light of his glory and grace

is word shall not fail you he promised
elieve him and all will be well
hen go to a world that is dying
is perfect salvation to tell

Turn your eyes upon Jesus
Look full in his wonderful face
And the things of earth will grow strangely dim
In the light of his glory and grace

O soul are you weary and troubled
No light in the darkness you see
There's light for a look at the Savior
And life more abundant and free

Turn your eyes upon Jesus
Look full in his wonderful face
And the things of earth will grow strangely dim
In the light of his glory and grace

We Gather Together

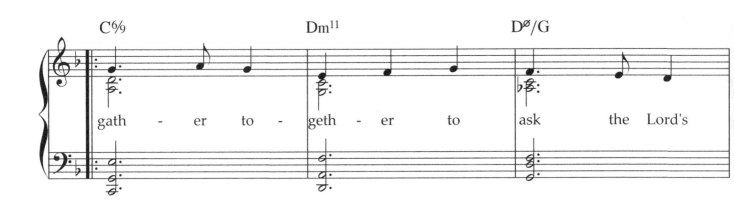

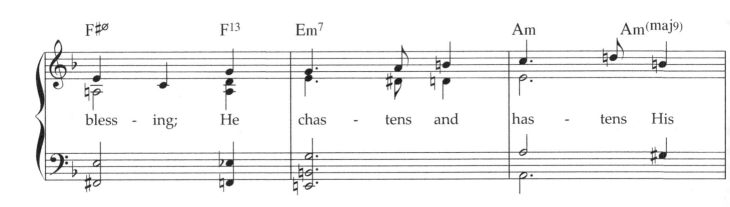

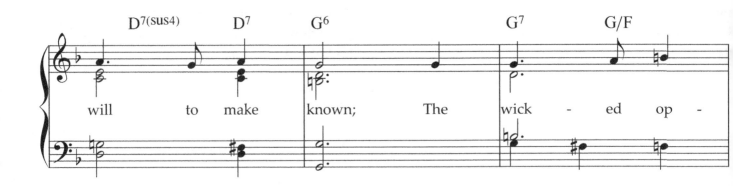

gather together to ask the Lord's blessing;
chastens and hastens His will to make known;
wicked oppressing now cease from distressing.
g praises to His name, He forgets not His own.

side us to guide us, our God with us joining,
daining, maintaining His kingdom divine;
from the beginning the fight we were winning:
Lord was at our side- the glory be Thine!

We all do extol Thee, Thou leader triumphant
and pray that Thou still our defender wilt be.
Let Thy congregation escape tribulation;
Thy name be ever praised! O Lord, make us free!

What a Friend We Have In Jesus

♩=160

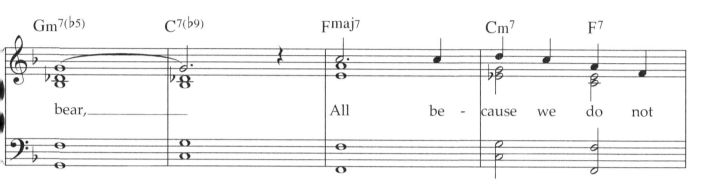

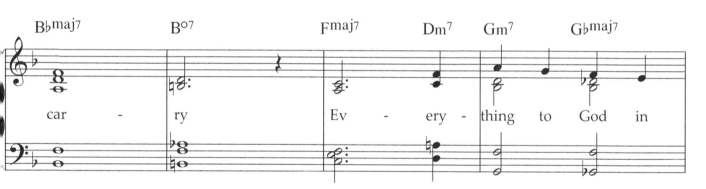

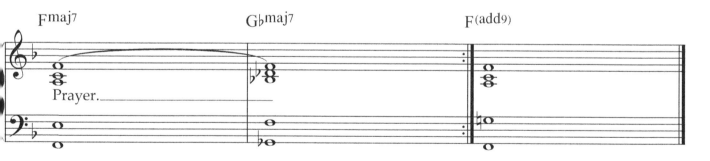

What a friend we have in Jesus
All our sins and griefs to bear
What a privilege to carry
everything to God in prayer!

O what peace we often forfeit
O what needless pain we bear
All because we do not carry
everything to God in prayer

Have we trials and temptations?
Is there trouble anywhere?
We should never be discouraged
Take it to the Lord in prayer

Can we find a friend so faithful
Who will all our sorrows share?
Jesus knows our every weakness
Take it to the Lord in prayer

When I Survey the Wondrous Cross

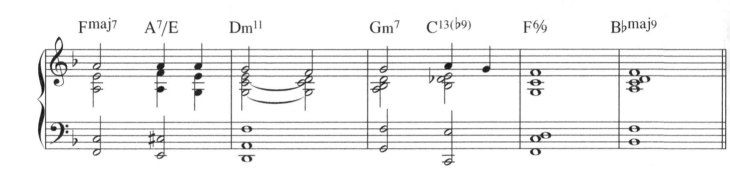

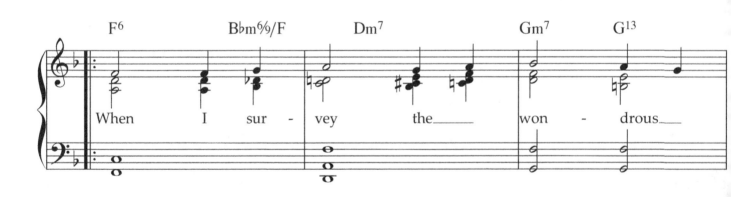

When I sur - vey the_____ won - drous_____

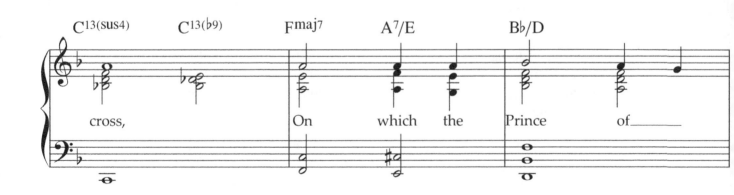

cross, On which the Prince of_____

When I survey the wondrous cross
On which the Prince of Glory died
My richest gain I count but loss
And pour contempt on all my pride

Forbid it Lord that I should boast
Save in the death of Christ my Lord
All the vain things that charm me most
I sacrifice them to His blood

See from His head His hands His feet
Sorrow and love flow mingled down
Did ever such love and sorrow meet
Or thorns compose so rich a crown

Were the whole realm of nature mine
That were an offering far too small
Love so amazing so divine
Demands my soul my life my all

Made in the USA
Las Vegas, NV
08 March 2024

86825819R00024